MW01278047

The Ultimate Social Media

"Larry Blumsack's book is a much-needed reminder of the original social medium—face-to-face connections in real time, with real people. *Face-to-Face is The Ultimate Social Media* takes the reader on a quest to discover and develop the qualities needed to forge true connection in the workplace and beyond."

> —*Daniel H. Pink, NY Times and WSJ bestselling author of*
> *A Whole New Mind and Drive*

"The social 'line' today is everything is happening on 'line'. The reality is, many times in business, we use the web to drive to the off-'line' face-to-face big sale! Blumsack has done a masterful job uniquely illustrating how to put your best socialFACE on."

> —*Jeff Taylor, Founder, monster.com*

"A powerful guide for building business revenue by creating relationships that count! With his straight-to-the-point strategies and tips for developing the five steps that will help you achieve meaningful, lasting connections, Larry Blumsack opens the door to attaining higher levels of success in business and life."

> —*Ivan Misner, NY Times bestselling author and*
> *Founder of BNI and Referral Institute*

"British Airways understands in-person meetings are crucial for businesses looking to expand. Larry Blumsack's fast-paced, timely book takes this one step further, offering tips to help people to embrace the true benefits of face-to-face interaction of any kind. Since technology can never take the place of shaking someone's hand, we designed our own Face-to-Face program to provide resources including education, advice and free travel for entrepreneurs to conduct critical meetings abroad. We encourage US entrepreneurs and small business owners to read this book! They stand to profit greatly from Larry's wisdom and advice."

> —*Simon Talling-Smith, Executive Vice President, Americas,*
> *British Airways*

"This book is for everyone and a very timely next-step to the One Minute Manager. In our increasingly virtual digital world, Blumsack's five steps are vital for anyone seeking to personally and emotionally bond face-to-face with others. My team of senior professionals and partners participated in one of his content-packed programs where he showed us how to take prior sales and business development trainings to another level. He even shook a few skeptics out of their comfort zone."

—Janice DiPietro, National Managing Partner,
Consulting Services, Tatum, LLC

"Face-to-Face is The Ultimate Social Media, master 'storyseller' Larry Blumsack delivers powerful insights that will help every professional go beyond casual online connection to authentic business relationships. Filled with wisdom and founded on decades of experience, this book provides an edge to everyone interested in personal and professional growth."

—Gary A. LaBranche, CAE, President & CEO,
Association for Corporate Growth®

"The story grabs you from the start and doesn't let you go until you 'get' it! A must read for young and old alike. It is what today's social networking is missing! A fun and easy-to-understand framework for excellent and productive relationships!"

—Dr. Beverly Edgehill, CEO, The Partnership

"At last—an antidote to this age of digital communicators! In this engaging, wise book, Larry Blumsack teaches us to use our minds rather than our thumbs to build meaningful bonds with people. A masterful communicator, he illuminates the marvel in face-to-face encounters. Larry taught me how to find my voice in political communications—as he has taught thousands of businessmen and women how to find their voices—how to stand out—as leaders. His message: mindful face-to-face interactions enrich the human spirit."

—Evelyn F. Murphy, Founder/President, The WAGE Project, Inc and
former Lt. Governor of Massachusetts

"Larry Blumsack's insightful book is right on target. I see my students' increasing dependence on Internet technology such as Facebook, LinkedIn and email to start and build successful careers. But as Larry points out, without the personal interaction skills, this technology will only get you so far. My MBA students realized this problem in an interactive seminar Larry conducted. It was a transformative experience for numerous students, and this book details the many critical lessons and the five steps they took away."

—Professor Todd Alessandri, Northeastern University College of Business Administration

"Whether you'd like a happier personal life or a more profitable professional life, Larry Blumsack's highly readable and hugely useful book will get you there. I can't tell you how much time I've spent online trying to absorb all I can about the wonders and the workings of social media. So I was greatly relieved when I found this slim little book—in print!—chock full of wit and wisdom about the 'ancient art' of face-to-face interaction. Read it, enjoy it, and profit from it!"

—Lynn A. Robinson, Bestselling author of Trust Your Gut: How the Power of Intuition Can Grow Your Business

"In our dizzying modern world of information overflow, Blumsack's book cuts through with clarity and precision. A valuable guide for how to develop relationships that transcends salesmanship and is applicable across all forms of interpersonal interactions."

—Jeffrey Bussgang, General Partner, Flybridge Capital Partners, and author of Mastering the VC Game

"Through wise and thoughtful prose, Larry Blumsack, the consummate 'Sales Guru' and 'StorySeller', delivers a powerful message that reminds the reader of the need to return to the long lost art of Face-to-Face communication by developing 5 steps that will enhance the development of professional and personal relationships – a refreshing commonsense counterbalance to our digital din!"

—John C. Jay, Managing Director, Executive Resources International, Boston's oldest executive search firm.

"Face-to-Face is The Ultimate Social Media packs a bang for a little book! A provocative distillation of wisdom about how to connect to others using almost forgotten principles of face-to-face engagement, it challenges us to rediscover looking, seeing, hearing, listening and opening ourselves emotionally and intuitively to others. It reminds us of the power of personal narratives in building relationships and gaining buy-in from others. It offers practical habits of mind that are central to selling ideas and exercising leadership. Face-to-Face is The Ultimate Social Media message is accessible, persuasive, practical and presented in an enormously entertaining way. It captures essential lessons about effective communication that Blumsack learned over more than four decades of diverse experiences ranging from sales to acting, and it does so using what he calls StorySelling. StorySelling harnesses elemental intra-personal and attitudinal skills that should be mastered by everyone wanting to successfully connect to others with powerful ideas. StorySellling gives the advantage of passion to communications that might otherwise be simply buried in the digital information's overload."

—*Edmund Barry Gaither, Director, National Center of Afro-American Artists and its Museum.*

for a win-win

Face-to-Face

is

The Ultimate Social Media

Larry Blumsack

Published by

Zoka Institute, LLC

Zoka Institute, LLC
FACE-TO-FACE
IS
THE ULTIMATE SOCIAL MEDIA

Published by
Zoka Institute, LLC
Belmont, Massachusetts

The term *Zoka Training* is a registered trademark used with the
permission of Larry Blumsack and the
Zoka Institute.

For information address:
Zoka Institute, LLC
9 Concord Avenue Suite B, Belmont, Massachusetts 02478
www.zokainstitute.com
www.larryblumsack.com
www.theultimatesocialmedia.com

To book Larry Blumsack for a speaking engagement, workshop or
coaching visit www.larryblumsack.com

Book cover and book design by Stephen Minor

Library of Congress Control Number: 2010936101

ISBN 978-0-9829882-0-6

Teach me and I shall forget.
Show me and I shall remember.
Let me do it and I shall understand.

Thich Nhat Hanh

Contents

"Seeking a Win-Win"

Introduction

What do you do to cultivate and bond relationships made through LinkedIn, Plaxo, Facebook, Twitter, Youtube, email or any form of social media? How do you connect with them? How do you get the sale?

The digital world of social media and Internet dramatically improves the speed and capability to reach out and connect with others. Today, the power to initially connect professionally or personally with someone is reduced to a mouse click. The press of a key on a keyboard or keypad.

But then what?

This book is for those interested in making the emotional connection necessary to foster and build strong, lasting relationships. People motivated to acquire or improve their skills to communicate effectively and successfully Face-to-Face in sales, in the workplace and in their lives.

Let's face it, business is done better Face-to-Face— when you know how. The essence of all successful business is relationship.

Personal and work worlds are merging and are increasingly virtual and mobile, resulting in dramatically reduced opportunities for and frequency of Face-to-Face interactions.

X and Y generations grew up on computer technology. They think, work and act visually, digitally and virtually. Today, greater challenges confront the development of social skills and Face-to-Face communications skills of the next generation.

Adults give children as young as 18 months old

smart phones, Kindles, iPads to foster accelerated self-learning skills.

Kindergarten to 8th grade, online, virtual schools are breeding a new generation of children across the U.S. who will lose even more valuable Face-to-Face contact and social-skill development during early education. We are raising cyberspace kids wired to think even more digitally and virtually than Gen X and Y.

Face-to-Face skills cannot be replaced with digital skills, in spite of the continuing, innovative, technology-driven paradigm shifts in business and personal cultures. Face-to-Face skills are the keys to emotionally and effectively connect with prospects. With anyone.

The first-person storytelling structure of this book is designed to place you in the shoes of the Seeker. To introduce you to the "Five Steps" necessary to be successful at StorySelling. StorySelling—the emotional speedway to the brain.

StorySelling paints a picture with words that an audience can visualize, internalize and connect with. People learn and retain far more when they can imagine—in their mind's eye—what is being presented.

The Seeker storytells each section of the book using descriptive, first-person narrative to help you to visualize in your mind's eye each of the encounters; show you the power of StorySelling; provide you with the tools to capture your audience's attention; and give you the Face-to-Face skills to captivate and connect emotionally with your listeners. To get the sale. To stand out in a highly commoditized, highly competitive marketplace.

"The practical techniques in this book are based on my hands-on experiences over 45 successful years of training thousands of sales and business development professionals and others. The "Five Steps" covered are the foundation of Zoka Training® and my ongoing presentations, workshops and mentoring programs. They are the mojo, the best-practices formula on how to stand out from the crowds. How to step out of your comfort zone. How to get the sale. How to win.

The goal of this book is to equip you with the concepts and tools to lead a richer and fuller life. To get the win-win. And remember....

> ***When it comes to Face-to-Face,***
> ***you possess the most powerful***
> ***social media tool of all.***
> ***YOU!***

The Seeker.

Early on, my parents and teachers instilled in me the desire to be the best. The best in anything and everything that I chose to do with my life. My passion for sales began at the age of six with my first lemonade stand in front of the house. I loved meeting and speaking with new people and convincing them I had the best solution for a hot day—and then convincing them they needed a refill as we chatted.

Every little business venture I launched or job I held through high school had something to do with sales. I sold more cookies, magazines, household items for school fund-raisers than any of my classmates.

In college, I decided to become the best-of-breed as a salesperson.

I consider myself a *Type A* personality. I earned an MBA. I completed popular training programs in sales, business development, presentation skills, negotiating, and personal development. However, I came to realize that I lacked sufficient competitive-edge skills to get to yes more frequently.

One day, I learned about a legendary salesman, the Sales Guru. They say he could sell snow to penguins in Antarctica. They say his genius stems from his charm as a crackerjack storyteller. He is a master at building meaningful and lasting relationships. He's also known to mentor others.

I decided if he is that good I need to find him and find a way to learn from him.

Eventually, I located him in Boston. Week after week I called, emailed, snail-mailed, even FedExed my request for a meeting. My middle name is Persistence.

Finally, I scored an appointment with the Sales Guru for 7:30 this morning. Now that I have the appointment my bravado is waning. In the mirrored elevator speeding up to the 22nd floor I look at myself. I feel intimidated and not quite sure how to approach this meeting.

I have no idea what he's like. Or even what he looks like. All I heard is that he's a charming, no-nonsense straight-shooter. What do I say? What do I ask?

Helen, his pleasant middle-aged secretary, ushers me into a light-filled, elegant yet simple and tastefully decorated office. There is no clutter. Contemporary paintings in muted pastel tones dominate the room. An exquisite hand-crafted oak desk stands out.

I'm struck by the lack of technology. No computer is visible nor or the typical clutter of chargers for smart phones and laptops. Not even a laptop.

I have no idea what to expect. All I know is he consistently closes major deals. He does it for software companies. He does it for computer-hardware companies. He does it for financial service companies. He's successful in many industries.

On the hour, this old guy enters the room. He's dressed in black slacks and a black turtleneck. This really sets off his wild white hair. His face is full and unlined. He moves with the ease and strength of a much younger man. I ask myself, "Is this character the Sales Guru?"

He sits down in his fancy chrome-trimmed Aeron chair. A powerful, resonant voice booms out, "The only reason I agreed to a meeting is because of your persistence. What are your expectations?"

To my surprise, I respond timidly. I can't grasp what

is going on for me because the last thing I am is timid. "I want to become a master at the art of sales."

He fixes his poker-face gaze on me and is silent for what seems like an eternity. I can't read him. I can't tell if he is offended, amused or angry.

The Sales Guru breaks the silence. "So you came looking for a solution on how to be the best. Are you familiar with the old story of the Royal Archer who travels a kingdom seeking complete mastery in archery? He too was seeking perfection and a competitive edge."

This is hardly the response I expected. I am puzzled. What does archery have to do with sales? I summon my strength and only eke out a soft "no."

He shifts, sits back in his chair, takes a slow deep breath, and begins,

"There was a famous archer, the best in the kingdom, who desired to shoot a perfect score every single time. He traveled throughout the land in search of anyone who could provide him with the knowledge of how to shoot perfect scores 100% of the time. The archer was an experienced and well-conditioned athlete. His six foot frame was muscular. He was square-jawed and handsome with an erect posture and determined stride.

One day, while rounding the bend of a winding dirt road lined with tall evergreens, a weathered red barn on the outskirts of a tiny village caught his eye. To his amazement, he found the side of the barn peppered with 12 arrows, each dead center in a separate bull's-eye.

He rushed into the nearby village looking for

the archer who was so accurate.

"Who," he asked some villagers, "is the master archer who hit the bull's-eyes every time on that red barn at the edge of town?"

Giggling, the villagers pointed to a disheveled, gnarly old man sleeping against the wall of a ramshackle house on the other side of the village. Clutched in his hand was a bent tree branch strung as a bow.

"You must be kidding?" was the quizzical response from the Royal Archer.

The villagers roared with laughter and hoots, and exclaimed almost in unison, "The expert you seek is the village Fool."

The Royal Archer thought, Fool or not, if this man can help me, I want to learn his secret."

Shaking the man in the tattered clothes awake, the Royal Archer asked, "Are you the archer who shot the arrows into the red barn?"

The Fool, rubbing his eyes, with a smirk on his deeply lined, aged face responded, "Yes, that was me."

The Royal Archer—amazed that this wreck of a man with a tree branch for a bow could be so accurate and never miss—said, "I would like to learn how to be as accurate as you. Will you show me?"

The Fool sat up, honored to be asked to teach this elegantly dressed, obviously royal personage. Grabbing the Royal Archer's hand he led him through the village to the red barn.

The villagers hooted uproariously as they

watched royalty and fool walk together side by side.

Finally, they reached the red barn with the 12 arrows scattered on the side, each dead center in a bull's eye.

"Are those yours?" asked the Royal Archer.

"Yes." nodded the Fool, with an ear-to-ear grin.

"Will you show me how to do that?"

"Yes," said the Fool giggling.

"First, show me how you shoot," requested the Fool. "Do you see that knothole on the side of a barn, it's a little above my height in the middle board. Let me see you shoot your arrows through that knothole."

The Royal Archer focused on the knothole, the size of a large walnut. He drew a deep breath each time and shot four arrows. The first two went cleanly through the knothole. However, the last two nicked the edge of the knothole as they skittered through. After the last release, the Royal Archer muttered, "It must be the wind." He looked at the Fool and said, "It must be the wind throwing my arrows off."

After a moment of silence, the Fool grinned and said, "Yes, it is the wind. It is the wind within you, throwing you off."

Dumbstruck, the Royal Archer asked, "What do you mean the wind within me? What enables you to be so accurate?"

The Fool only smiled.

The Royal Archer asked, "How are you able

to be so accurate?"

The Fool added, "First, I shot the arrows into the side of the barn, and then I painted a bull's-eye around each arrow."

The Sales Guru finishes the story and asks, "Do you understand?"

Puzzled, I respond, "Sorry, no, I don't."

His eyes fix on me. He leans forward and whispers, "I want you to sit still in silence with no agenda—no mental multi-tasking, no gibberish, no monkey chatter in your mind. Take a few moments to tame your mind and then see if you understand."

I can't silence my mind. Numerous thoughts keep running through it. I came here to learn from the Sales Guru, and he has me sitting here in silence. I don't grasp the sense of the archer story. How is this going to help me be the best-of-breed in sales? Chatter, chatter, chatter. If there's a key to silencing my mind I'd love to know what it is.

Finally, he breaks the silence. "Like the Royal Archer, you come seeking a solution outside of yourself. Like him you don't search within yourself to examine what the real obstacle is. Like the Royal Archer, the real wind is within you. The change you seek must come from within."

The real obstacle is within you.

"But how do I discover what the obstacle is?" I stutter.

Then, without hesitation, I start rattling off a list of my abilities and successes. "As you recognized earlier, I am persistent. I have gone through many of the top sales and presentation-skills training programs. My sales numbers are always higher than the other members of teams I've been on.

"I am very skilled in social media, connected to 480 people on LinkedIn, and another 250 people in Plaxo. My Twitter followers number over 950. I'm connected to an additional 200 people on Facebook. I blog weekly, text message. Send out monthly e-mail newsletters, and network...."

"Yes, and I understand the need for all that." The Sales Guru pauses, "What Face-to-Face skills do you possess?"

Stunned, I am unable to answer.

"What personal assets do you have that separate you from your competition in your highly commoditized marketplace? What *mojo* do you command besides your arsenal of digital tools? What training have you done on how to effectively communicate and emotionally connect with a prospect?"

Looking him in the eye, I ask, "Is that the key to your success? If so, then that's exactly what I'm seeking. I want to learn what gifts you possess which enable you to connect with so many people and to be so successful."

His face looks stern, he answers, "It's not my skills, nor is it my gifts that will enable you to be successful. You are your own master.

"You are a prisoner of technology, your Blackberry, iPhone, Android or whatever. You are on speed. Like so many, you run to get places as fast as you possibly can without any thought of how or why you need to get there. Or for that matter, you are not giving any thought to what's preventing you from getting there. Look within yourself for the answers. As Albert Einstein said, 'We can't solve problems by using the same kind of thinking we used when we created them.'"

We can't solve problems by using the same kind of thinking we used when we created them. Einstein

He rears back in his chair and tells me, "You are a victim of an industrial-age educational system. A system that teaches one from kindergarten through PhD—no you can't, here's the answer, fear the judgments of others, be serious, and don't make mistakes."

"Now, on top of all of that logical, linear, sequential, analytical teaching and thinking, we add on a new phenomenon called social media. You may be a whiz at video games, tweeting, blogging, text messaging, and all the digital tools and strategies available today. I grant you that properly used social media and the Internet are important tools for successful sales and business development."

"There's no question as far as I'm concerned," I interject, "of the Internet's value in narrowing down targets and researching prospects. Today, it's all about the ability to connect quickly with someone else and…"

The Sales Guru interrupts, "One's ability to connect in person is what is really important. I agree that digital and social media are great tools to narrow down who you want to connect to. However, what actually matters is who is listening. Let's face it, when it comes to getting to yes, Face-to-Face is the ultimate social media. You and you alone are your most powerful media."

What actually matters is who is listening. You are your most powerful media.

"There is no mold for a sales leader or for any leader for that matter. Each individual must build on his or her own uniquenesses—on his or her own personal intellectual assets—on his or her own resources. Like the Archer, your mastery is buried deep within you. Finding those resources is akin to mining for diamonds or gold. You have to drill way down and dig deep to find them. You will never succeed by imitating anyone.

"Build from your own strengths and abilities. Be true to yourself. Be self-aware and listen to your own thoughts. Learn to trust your gut."

Moved by these comments I respond, "I'm open to learn. I deeply desire that competitive edge. Will you teach me the skills that made you so successful?"

The Sales Guru sits silently breathing deeply. He stares straight at me. The longer he sits without speaking or moving the tenser I become. Scattered thoughts swirl around in my head: Will he help me? What am I doing here? What is it I need to learn? All he has told me is a story about an archer seeking perfection.

I try again, "Will you mentor me?"

Finally, he moves without speaking. Opens his desk drawer. Removes a pad of lined paper and a wooden yellow pencil and proceeds to write. The sound of a pencil scratching against the paper is out of place in this contemporary office. He stands up and pushes the paper across the desk and says. "If you are serious about conquering the wind...."

With that, he strides out of the room. No goodbye. No handshake. He leaves me sitting there with a piece of paper in my hand.

I stare at dust motes floating in the shaft of sunlight streaming through the window. That warm light is a stark contrast to the Sales Guru's cold exit.

Finally, I read the paper:

Cory Stuart

21 Beacon Street

Boston

One hour from now.

Discover and build from your own strengths and your own assets.

Engage Mindfulness

I stand in front of one of Boston's historic three-story brownstones with an ornately carved front door and a polished brass lion-head door knocker. I have absolutely no idea who I am meeting and what his relationship is with the Sales Guru. Have I been sent on a wild goose chase by an old guy with wild white hair?

The entrance hall is ornate, with paneling and a decorated plaster ceiling. On the wall are a doorbell and a brass card holder with a card reading: Cory Stuart - Please Ring the Bell. Responding to my ring a resonant male voice through the speaker asks me to please go to the second floor and make myself comfortable.

I climb the carpeted stairs and open the door to find a very simple and spacious contemporary living room with white walls, an Oriental carpet, a comfortable leather couch, a big leather easy chair, and a low glass coffee table with a vase of fresh daisies. Two huge paintings hang side by side, covering most of one wall.

The left painting is filled with the energy and excitement of a multi-colored band of wild horses jumping, running and rearing sending a cloud of dust into the air. A whirlwind of motion across a plain. To the right in sharp contrast to the first painting, is a canvas of a lone Palomino serenely grazing in a lush green pasture.

I am startled when a distinguished, tall, middle-aged man enters the room. He has chiseled facial features and a shock of styled silver hair. He is casually, but expensively dressed in grey slacks, burgundy turtleneck and brown suede jacket. He shakes my hand, introduces himself as Cory Stuart and sits down in the chair opposite me.

In a smooth voice he says, "Let's sit here in silence for two minutes with no agenda."

So here I am just sitting again. All kinds of thoughts race through my mind, "Why am I here? What is this all leading to?" My head is filled with babble. I think about my meeting with the Sales Guru. I think maybe I'm wasting my time. There is no way I can sit in silence across from a stranger with no agenda.

Cory Stuart interrupts the silence. His words are measured. "Pay attention to your breath. Focus on breathing in and breathing out, in – out, in – out."

I'm not sure why but I comply. After a few moments I hear only my and Cory's breathing. Then, as quickly as the silence began, the yakkedy yak in my head comes back. I wonder, again, "What is this all about? Where is this all leading?"

Eventually, I ask, "Cory, who are you? What do you do? What is this all about? Why was I sent here?"

"I'm a mindfulness trainer," he calmly responds. "Are you familiar with mindfulness?"

Mindfulness trainer? I ask myself. What does this have to do with sales skills?

I think for a moment and then say, "I believe it has something to do with stress reduction and helping heal yourself when you're ill?"

Again silence.

Then Cory says calmly, slowly, softly, "That's a good start. It's about being fully present in the moment, non-judgmental and paying attention on purpose."

"This sounds pretty touchy-feely," I say

uncomfortably. "I'm puzzled and curious as to how this plays a role in my becoming a top salesperson like the Sales Guru."

Again silence. Then Cory says, "In reality we only live in the present moment. However, in our heads we live in the past and in the future at the same time, while rapidly skipping over or ignoring the present. Mindfulness and mindfulness training grew in popularity here in the U.S. toward the end of the 20th century. Its use began initially in hospitals and clinics, to help patients reduce the stress of their illnesses in a positive fashion.

"Today, business leaders, ranging from boards of directors down to all levels of workers in companies from General Mills to Google are engaged in mindfulness training. So are court judges, all ranks of military personnel, law enforcement detectives, hospital doctors and staff, and companies under fire from the public. They want to learn how to be non-judgmental, how to be fully present in the present moment. They want to pay attention 'on purpose.' They also realize the significant benefits of mindfulness in reducing the stress of daily life."

Cory pauses, "Now do you see how these are ideal goals for business development and sales professionals?"

I take a minute to absorb what Cory just laid out. "I can see how it can make sense. Still, it sounds very new age."

"There is nothing new age about mindfulness," Cory continues, "Mindfulness and mindfulness training, used in a much broader sense, have been a staple in Eastern cultures for centuries—Tibet, India, China, and Japan, for example.

"Mindfulness enables you to tune in to what resonates with others. It starts with self-awareness, with learning how to turn off your limiting habit energy which developed over the years, in order to better perceive what is going on in the moment. Whether it's an interview, sales presentation, conference, meeting, sales pitch—or even a date."

"What do you mean, 'limiting habit energy'?"

"Your quick, knee-jerk response based on years of acquiring and harboring ingrained and reactive habits."

"So, how is mindfulness used?"

"It's learning how to perceive things with greater accuracy. It's having the right view. It's not prejudging or being judgmental in the presence of others while keeping an open mind. Pre-judgment is a major roadblock to successful personal interaction.

"It's crucial to understand the difference between perception and deception. Don't be fooled by what you think you perceive, because if you are not fully present your perceptions tend to be erroneous. Our years of habit thinking tend to supersede our present thinking. Simply, we don't see clearly."

Perceptions tend to be erroneous.

"A mindful approach requires less energy and is more accurate, rewarding, and effective than a mindless one," he continues. "We spend too much time thinking mindlessly and mentally multitasking. As a result of today's technology our workday is endless. We work everywhere—in the office, while traveling, at home, and on vacation. We work 24/7 with no beginning or end to the work week."

"Are you pointing out what the Sales Guru attempted to get me to understand? That it all starts by conquering the wind within me?"

Cory smiles, "Succinctly phrased. Leave it to the Sales Guru to cut to the chase. Now, let's move forward.

"You need to learn to focus on your breath and how to trust your gut. In other words, trust your own experiences. Discover your own wisdom."

"How?"

"Let's examine what we have to undo. Let's discover and understand your problems before we come up with solutions. People spend too much time fearing and worrying about the judgment of others, and making mistakes. Being too serious. We are a civilization on speed. Speeding on computers, iPhones, Blackberries, iPods, iPads, broadband cards and being digitally connected. The digital world is on fire but doesn't know it. People are burning up from information overload."

I shake my head, "I am reluctant to agree."

"We are so addicted to gadgets and mechanisms we don't bother to think anymore." Cory continued, "We push a button that tells us what to do and how to do it. We push a button to spell check and grammar check. Yet, there's no button to spell check and grammar check speech. We can't be effective racing to be efficient by multitasking, and burning the candle at both ends. The enemy of mindfulness and innovation is speed.

"Studies have shown that runaway multitasking leads to a loss of effectiveness. The loss of effectiveness can be as high as 30 or 40%."

Much of the world is on speed.

"You make an excellent point. On the other hand, society puts enormous pressure on us to multi-task. How do you break away?"

Cory pauses, "Knowing how to be effective will separate you from the competition, from all the other people who can do what you can do as well as you can do it. Being efficient gets in the way. Learn how to push your own buttons. First you need to learn what buttons you have to push."

"Well presented. I think I get it. I can see the value of being mindful. So often I walk into a meeting with a fixed agenda and pre-judgment about the people. How and where do I begin?" I ask eager to learn.

"Today, I can only provide you with starters and point you in the right direction. Once you're on the right path you will need to practice, practice, practice. The professional and personal benefits are many.

"Begin by mindfully focusing on simple daily activities with no mental multi-tasking. Don't think about the past or the future. Forget about the talking points of an upcoming meeting or presentation.

"Completely focus on the individual task at hand as you brush your teeth, wash your hands, prepare food, drive a car, take a breath, eat an apple, wait in line, ride an elevator, walk, run, or sip a drink. These are starters you can easily incorporate into your daily life.

I'm feeling overwhelmed. "That's a major lifestyle change for me."

"I also recommend you spend 10 minutes a day writing down—and I do mean writing down—the questions and issues that challenged your mindfulness that day.

"For guidance there are numerous quality mindfulness books and audio programs you can purchase.

"To take mindfulness to another level, start by meditating daily for 5 to 10 minutes guided by an audio meditation program. Work towards a daily meditation of 20 to 30 minutes. Some people prefer to meditate first thing in the morning, and others in the evening. And never meditate when you're driving." he says with a chuckle.

Laughing I say, "Don't worry I won't drive and meditate! But what am I trying to achieve by being mindful?"

Cory leans forward, smiles and says, "In time, you will learn to tame the multi-tasking beast in you. Practice will liberate you from bad habit energy and linear thinking. You will learn how to become non-judgmental and pay attention on purpose in the present moment. As other thoughts come up, don't fight them, just let them pass through. Return to focusing on your breath. That's an important step in learning to conquer the wind within you."

Cultivate the abilities to see clearly and to be more objective.

Quizzically, I ask, "How did you and the Sales Guru connect?"

Cory stands up and walks to the painting of the Palomino. Looking at the painting he says, "It was a number of years ago at the gym. One day he commented to me about how calm I always appeared. He envied me because of the stress he was under on a daily basis. The Sales Guru and I ended up working intensely together for over a year. We still meet at least once a month."

"What's the possibility of me working with you?"

Cory looks me over and responds, "Who knows, maybe we will end up doing that. First, there are more steps for you to go through before anything can be determined."

"More steps! Such as?" I ask.

He points to the two large paintings on the wall and tells me that my job is to learn to become as mindful as the lone Palomino grazing in the pasture. He tells me that I alone control the choices of where to place my attention.

"Learn to treat every red light, phone ring, horn beep and elevator ride as a signal. A signal to take three deep breaths to bring yourself fully into the present moment. Take three breaths before you make a phone call. Before you send an e-mail. Before you enter a room. Before you speak. Learn to tame the wind in your mind by concentrating on a word or an object. The key to Face-to-Face is to relax and focus on the entire person or persons you face. It's one way to center yourself."

Cory tells me to think back to when I was a child absorbed in play, oblivious to anything else. "For children being fully present and mindful is a natural state. Speeding through life, we lose that ability to focus intensely on the here and now. With mindfulness training, one can regain the ability to be as focused, relaxed, and present as that happy child."

He hands me a sheet of paper, says "She's expecting you this afternoon," smiles, firmly shakes my hand and leaves me sitting in the room, staring at the painting of the grazing Palomino. I wonder what it will take for me to gain that level of calmness and equanimity.

I sit quietly, paying attention to my breath. Breathing in and breathing out. Captured by the image of the Palomino, and fully aware of my breath, my shoulders begin to relax. Slowly, my face and hands relinquish their tension. I feel peaceful and calm. Wow! I can do it!

Be Mindful

Be Fully Present

No Prejudgment

Relax

Focus

Look and See

Now, I'm puzzled more than ever. That afternoon my next stop is with Andrea Kurezci at the Isabella Stewart Gardner Museum.

A quick search on my iPhone provides information on the museum. It is housed in the stunning 15th-century Venetian-style palace I'm facing. Andrea Kurezci shows up as an art curator. I wonder what role an art curator can play in developing great sales skills.

The officious security guard at the entrance calls in my presence and a few minutes later a rusty haired, heavy-set, plain, but intense woman in a dark blue business suit barrels in and introduces herself as Andrea Kurezci. She grabs my hand with a vice-like grip and vigorously pumps it up and down. Speaking quickly, in a no-nonsense and gravelly voice, she leads me into the galleries.

"I trust your meeting with Cory Stuart was beneficial. He trains and coaches business leaders of Fortune 500 corporations on how to be mindful. Let's see how much you've learned."

I feel a bit defensive and respond, "Isn't it a bit premature for me to practice what I was just introduced to a few hours ago?"

In a stern tone Andrea says, "Why is it premature? You appear to be intelligent. It's never premature to start changing habit energy. Ask the Sales Guru."

I confess. "I don't yet know how to be mindful."

"Then this will be an opportunity for you to practice," she replies tersely. "It is never too early to practice paying attention on purpose and be fully present in the moment with no monkey chatter."

We enter a long narrow, dark passage. There is a solid wall on the right and a colonnade on the left leading to an indoor court yard. The space reminds me of a chapel. At the end of the room there is a large painting. I later learn that the gallery was built specifically to showcase this 11 foot wide, 8 foot high painting.

"What do you see?" Andrea challenges me.

"I see a woman in a long ruffled skirt prancing around."

Andrea informs me, "You respond like every police officer, FBI agent, Homeland Security trainee, or medical student I've worked with. In the simplest of terms you are correct. Your eye went directly to the dominant image in the painting. But you didn't see anything significant."

"Where should I be looking?"

She continued, "You did what I call jumping to a conclusion. You looked yet you didn't really see. You didn't pay attention on purpose."

Andrea Kurezci is sounding like a clone of Cory Stewart. I'm hearing a recurring theme.

You need to pay attention on purpose.

"You did what the Sales Guru did the first time we met," Andrea says. "When you first encounter a scene, whether it's this painting, a fire disaster, a murder scene, a sales meeting, or a job interview, you will gain far more knowledge of the situation by taking the time to scan and observe the entire scene before making any assessment."

I back up several steps to view the painting again.

"Think about a play or movie you've seen," continues Andrea, "or book you've read. Early on you get a sense of the setting or location, enabling you to obtain an overall grasp of the situation. Let's apply the same principle to a sales meeting, or for that matter, any type of meeting or situation. Taking in the entire scene is step one in learning to *look and see*. If you stay the course with us eventually you will meet someone who will go into more depth on the outline I am about to provide."

Stay the course with us. What was it Cory said? There are more steps in the process. I can't stop wondering what's in store for me after this visit.

Andrea steps beside me and resumes, "Look at the painting again and tell me what you see. Take in the entire painting. Start to *look and see*. Try to be fully present. Take deep breaths, breathing in and out."

The breathing part is easy. But being fully present is another story for me.

I take my time to scour the entire painting. Eventually I say, "This is some type of rustic tavern or café. It is dark, filled with male musicians sitting in chairs against the wall on the left. On the right a group of women appear to be joyously and energetically dancing. The central figure is a woman who could be walking or dancing."

Suddenly, I have an "aha" moment. I realize, based on the shadows high up on the wall and the way the flowing gown is lit from below that the light sources are on the floor.

Gaining confidence I continue, "Maybe this is a stage and the central figure is performing for an unseen audience. Based on the clothing, it appears the artist captured a scene from Mexico or Spain in the seventeen or eighteen hundreds."

"You just learned an important step required to become best-of-breed. You paid attention on purpose to *look and see* and established a whole-view starting point. This practice of setting the location is important in any presentation, meeting or situation. Learn to take in the whole scene when you first enter a place you've never been before. It can also apply to a place you've been. It's a learned skill. Practice it long and hard enough and eventually you will *look and see* in a blink.

Look and see.

"Good job—you established the setting reasonably well. You are a quick learner. Now describe the characters."

I decide to break the painting down into three groups, leaving the solo woman in the flowing dress for last.

"Several musicians are seated against the wall on the left. They are dressed in black and either clapping or playing guitars. They are expressionless. One person sits with hands in his lap, head thrust back and mouth wide open. I can't tell if he is sleeping or in ecstasy. On the right, colorfully dressed young women are enthralled, happily and energetically dancing. It's clear to me the central character is also dancing. She is a confident, joyous and sensual solo dancer on stage. My guess— based on the setting, the musicians, and her posture— she is performing a flamenco dance."

"Excellent!" cries Andrea. "You analyzed it quicker than most men do; even quicker than the Sales Guru the first time he saw the painting. You told the story of this painting."

"Back to the painting," she persists, "You have captured the essence of John Singer Sargent's famous painting *El Jaleo*. He was a world-renowned painter who spent years immersed in the culture of Spain."

Suddenly, I have another "aha" moment. I realize having something interesting and specific to concentrate on enables me to subdue my scattered thinking and view the painting with more clarity.

"Now, tell me what did you hear?" she asks.

"Whoa! What did I hear?" I ask in amazement. "It's a painting!"

"Yes, it's a painting," she fiercely shoots back, "and paintings convey emotions, feelings, and in this case, music as well. If you approach everything you do using six senses you will make the emotional connection necessary to build any type of relationship."

"Wait a minute! Did you say six senses? I only know of five."

Andrea fires back with, "The five senses of sight, hearing, taste, feel and smell are tied to a sixth sense known as mind sense. More specifically the sixth sense is about awareness. ***Whole-body thinking*** is our ability to think with our entire body by using all senses. All six of them! Advances in neuroscience through magnetic resonance imaging (MRI) confirm that the more we're in touch with all of our senses, the more facile and imaginative our thinking is.

"Too often we look, but don't see; listen but don't hear; breathe, but don't smell; eat, but don't taste. And we touch, but don't feel. Speed is the enemy of being present and *whole-body thinking.* You will learn that in business the senses make cents."

The senses make cents.

"People need to get out of their heads and start using all of the innate, creative and intellectual assets and gifts they possess, by using all six senses to think. Most visual and performing artists have known this for centuries. It is nice to finally have it scientifically confirmed through MRI. That's *whole-body thinking*. So what did you hear?" Andrea snaps back.

She's tough but I'm game. I close my eyes and try to put myself in a Spanish cabaret. I am not that familiar with flamenco music. Clearly guitars play an important role in this painting. If I remember correctly, it is the clicking of heels which is integral to flamenco dancing. Instantly the monkey chatter in my head starts up again.

I hear Cory in my head. Breathe in. Breathe out. As I start to focus on breathing I come back into the present. "I can hear some laughter, hands clapping and guitars playing. You know, Andrea, I believe I am starting to understand what you mean by *whole-body thinking*. I can see applying this to sales presentations."

"There's much more for you to learn in order to fully grasp the concept and to practice *whole-body thinking*. You've only been exposed to two steps on the path to being present and attentive. *Engage mindfulness* and *look and see* are two critical tools in getting to yes.

"In any sales meeting, presentation, group meeting, job interview or personal interaction it is critical to be able to quickly—with an open mind, pay attention with purpose—assess the entire scene and the motivation of people. Often the key player or decision-maker present is not the best-dressed or the most prominent figure, or even the person who organized the meeting."

"Is it the *look and see* you talk about that will provide me that skill?"

"I'll give you an example," Andrea goes on. "There was a recent study done with medical students on how they improved their observation skills. They were broken into two groups. One group went to the local museum a half-day a week for several weeks. A curator and doctors taught them how to analyze paintings and sculptures, to assess and try to determine the physical and emotional state of the painted or sculpted people they were looking at. By learning how to *look and see* this group improved their overall patient observation skills at the hospital by 30-40% over students in a control group who did not receive arts-based observation skills training."

"That's impressive."

"You're darn right. Think about what you've just learned about this painting with a two-step guideline. First and foremost, establish the location in detail. Go on to describe the characters in detail. Practice it often enough and eventually you will learn to *look and see* in a blink. That blink will provide your competitive edge.

"That blink will provide you with the knowledge and ability to know what—and who—is important in a situation...and why."

Look and see in a blink.

"Andrea, any other tips for me?"

She looks thoughtful, "Spend time looking in museums, art galleries, nature and public places," she advises. "Be an observer in meetings where you are not presenting. Whenever you can, analyze people for physical and mental attributes. These are ways to sharpen your ability to ***look and see***."

"To this day," she continues, "The Sales Guru is a frequent visitor here, as well as at the Museum of Fine Arts across the way."

"I'm curious as to how you two met."

"He contacted me after reading a magazine article about my teaching police detectives how to ***look and see***. He asked me to coach him, which I do to this day."

"Wow, he does? Any other advice?" I ask.

"Use your eyes like a zoom lens. Start with a wide-angle view and slowly zoom in as you pan from side-to-side. This technique will enable you to determine where your close-up focal point should be.

"Think of the valuable information you will gain applying this technique when you are fully present, Face-to-Face with a group or one person. Think of it as a whole body scan to discover what is under the façade.

"Remember, the most obvious is not necessarily the most important. The ability to really see in a blink takes practice, practice, practice."

The most obvious is not necessarily the most important.

With that final comment, she bids me farewell in the same fashion that Cory did before her. Andrea Kurezci simply hands me a piece of paper and leaves me in the gallery, staring at *El Jaleo*.

Look and See

Be Mindful

Be Fully Present

No Prejudgment

Relax

Focus

Listen and Hear

Boston Symphony Hall is the next morning's destination, to meet with Ron Fiedler. Another mystery. Who is Fiedler and what role does he play in this developing puzzle?

When I arrive at Symphony Hall, a grumpy, lumpy, security guard at the door tells me Fiedler is in rehearsal. He quickly ushers me inside and seats me in the middle of the vast hall.

I remember reading that Symphony Hall is one of a few acoustically perfect music halls in the world. As I look around there is lot of red velvet and gold leaf. Two tiers of balconies cover the sides and back of the hall. Full figure, white marble statues, occupy niches in the sides and back walls above the top balcony. The ceiling must be at least 40-50 feet high. The stage is plain, except for massive organ pipes on the back wall. An eerie feeling creeps over me when I realize I'm the only one in the audience of this vast concert hall.

On stage, a slight, youthful, sandy-haired man in khakis and a blue button-down shirt instructs about 30 or 40 casually dressed musicians on the emphasis he's seeking in the next passage. I assume he is the conductor. The brass instruments sparkle as light bounces off of them. The conductor takes the podium, and with a wave of his baton the orchestra begins.

I sit listening, and thinking of Cory and Andrea, and try to concentrate to be fully present in the moment as I *look and see.*

It is a struggle to tame the wild horses stampeding around in my head, while I attempt to take in the full scene before me. Flashing through my mind is, which person, if any of them, is Ron Fiedler? The grouchy security guard didn't tell me anything. Does Fiedler play violin, trumpet, horn, percussion, or the harp? Is he the conductor? Is he even part of the orchestra? What role did he or does he play in the life of the Sales Guru? What's the significance to meeting him in Symphony Hall?

On the other hand, each successive visit has provided me with a bit more insight into the tools that enabled the Sales Guru to become idolized as the master salesman.

I am astonished when I look at my watch. I have been sitting here for 20 minutes attempting to listen to my breath amidst the mixture of monkey chatter and orchestra sounds. There were moments of success, when I felt fully present. The success was fleeting, but at least a success.

A moment later, the conductor dismisses the orchestra for a break. Several members, along with the conductor walk up the aisle in my direction. As they pass, some smile. Some look quizzical. The young conductor approaches running his fingers through his thick long hair and introduces himself as Ron Fiedler.

"How did you like the music," he asks?

"I know little about classical music. I'm sorry I couldn't focus on it."

"It shouldn't be difficult to sit in this magnificent hall and focus on music."

Defensively, I tell him, "I was trying to tame the multitasking beast from taking me over."

"Listen to learn, not to defend," Ron softly responds. "We are going to continue rehearsal in 10 minutes. I'll return shortly. While you're waiting, practice sitting here quietly with no agenda. Practice listening to the music of your breath."

Listen to learn, not to defend.

Listen to learn, not to defend. Easier said than done, I think.

"I would like you to concentrate on the music when we start. First, take in the entire piece of music, then tune into the different instruments and groups of instruments to determine their roles in the passage. ***Listen and hear*** the different tones, tempos, rhythms and colors coming from the various parts of the orchestra, and from the whole orchestra. ***Listen and hear***," he repeats.

I expect this will be a daunting challenge.

On his way back from the break, Ron asks if I know how to differentiate the sounds of different instruments and instrument groups.

"I think I'll be able to figure out most of them, but don't ask me to tell you what they are. I know the difference between a clarinet and a sax. On the other hand, I have no idea what the differences are between a violin and what's called a viola."

"You don't have to be fluent in the language of music to recognize the roles that instruments play in a composition. Your goal this morning is to ***listen and hear***." Ron heads for the stage.

So that's my goal. That's why I'm here—to ***listen and hear***. On the surface it sounds so simple. ***Listen and hear***.

When the music starts I realize I am faced with a significant task. There are 30 to 40 musicians—some with several instruments. I am to distinguish the instruments and determine their roles in the piece. Attempting this with a small jazz ensemble would be so much easier for me.

Later, when Ron and I talk, he reminds me that in sales, most meetings or situations encountered are not ones with which I would be familiar. It's important to be nimble and to ***listen and hear*** regardless of the circumstances.

I try to be fully present and pay attention to the music. Again, having something specific to focus on—like viewing the painting *El Jaleo*—makes it easier to pay attention on purpose. The more I concentrate on listening the more I can pick out variations and subtleties from the various instruments. The longer I listen the more I enjoy the piece. The music possesses magical and lyrical qualities in contrast to some dark, low tone passages. As I think about it, I begin to realize that knowing how to ***listen and hear*** can be very important and relevant to a sales professional or for any Face-to-Face interaction. Eventually, I think I recognize the music as a theme from the movie *Fantasia.*

Ron dismisses the orchestra, and walks back and sits opposite me. He motions to me not to speak. We sit in silence for several minutes. In my head I work on preparing my answers to what I think he is going to ask.

"What did you hear?" he finally asks.

I couldn't wait, "Was this music from *Fantasia?* "

Ron was surprised at my response. "Yes, and only partially correct. The selection is *The Rite of Spring* by Russian composer Igor Stravinsky. Most people recognize it as bits of music they heard in *Fantasia*. Do you remember the movie?"

I think for a moment, "Somewhat."

"So what did you hear?

"Well over time, I was able to distinguish different instruments and groups of instruments."

"What did you hear?" he asks again.

"I'm not quite sure what you are asking."

"I'd like to know what you heard," Ron insists.

"I could tell when the string instruments were dominant, or a particular brass was dominant, or the percussion was featured, and I could also pick out instrument solos."

Ron chuckles, "For the last time," he firmly asks, "what did you hear?"

"I am still not sure what you're asking."

"Think of music as an intricate, colorful tapestry, expertly woven together to create a whole piece," explains Ron. "I just gave you several minutes of silence. That should have been sufficient time for you to reflect on what you heard. It was a good time to collect everything into one piece. Did you take the opportunity to do that?"

"Well no," I respond. "I was concerned about what questions you were going to ask and how to answer them."

"What you just said is typical—typical of anyone who goes to a meeting prepared to second-guess what people are going to ask or say.

"It never ceases to amaze me why we try to figure out how to answer questions that haven't been asked.

Learn to keep an open mind and to be fully present with your antennae up, poised in the right direction to *listen and hear*. That is more powerful and productive than listening to mindless projections in your head.

"Mindful hearing—developing the skills to *listen and hear*—allows you to transcend your world and participate in the world of others. Mindful hearing allows you to bring intuition and instinctive reaction into play. Some summarize this as right concentration."

"What do you mean by right concentration?"

"Active and selective are the two types of right concentration. Listening to what's happening in the present moment is active concentration. Paying attention to the entire orchestra playing or everything happening in a meeting is active concentration. Choosing one object—one instrument, one person—and concentrating on it is selective concentration.

"*Listen and hear* stems from right concentration. That's how to build and strengthen relationships. That's how to get to yes."

Listen and hear.

"Okay, I think it makes sense."

"What did you see and feel?" asks Ron.

"I saw the orchestra members playing their instruments and you conducting. And frankly, I felt somewhat inadequate, because I know so little about classical music."

"You can do better than that," Ron insists. "You recognized it as music from *Fantasia*. Did you see the movie?"

"Yes I did."

"If you contemplate the music and, if necessary close your eyes, you will find music can create images for you. Some people do it without closing their eyes. They do it by using their inner-vision."

I'm perplexed. "What is inner-vision?"

"Inner-vision is what we see projected in our mind's eye, as opposed to outer-vision, which is what we actually see in our field of view. One's ability to visualize comes from inner-vision.

"Music and words can stir a full range of emotions, which often result in a host of visualizations—images we can project in our mind's eye. Music is able to take you to mountain tops, float you down rivers, put you in grand ballrooms, or take you deep into the Grand Canyon. Let's use *The Right of Spring* suite in *Fantasia* as an example."

"Okay with me."

"In the movie, Stravinsky's music serves as a pulsing and driving background to a snapshot from Earth's formation to the extinction of the dinosaurs. Earth explodes into volcanoes spewing fire and flowing lava. Storm clouds burst open releasing torrents of rain. Oceans form. Cooled by the oceans, land masses develop. Numerous living organisms slowly evolve into flying, water, and land creatures. Picture the lumbering Triceratops, and the carnivorous Tyrannosaurus Rex. Eventually, all living creatures die. Their bones lie strewn all over Earth. A fiery sun sets as it drops behind a desolate planet. Fade to black."

"Wow! Some story! Nice Job! You certainly painted

a number of pictures I could envision." Still mesmerized by Ron's storytelling I ask, "Why couldn't I see any images as I listened to the orchestra?"

"You weren't listening with your whole body. You didn't allow the music to enter you. You didn't use all of your senses—all six of them—to emotionally connect with the music. Doing so will allow your mind to create its own images."

Slowly, I'm beginning to understand what the sixth sense is and how Ron's applying it.

Ron advises, "You have the innate skills required to *listen and hear* every day, with all types of music: street sounds, wind sounds, room sounds, nature sounds, and especially conversations. Wherever you are, *listen and hear*. Too many sales professionals suffer from diarrhea of the mouth. They are over eager, anxious to provide solutions with little or no knowledge of the real problems or issues right under their nose."

"I've been there—done that," uncomfortable, I sadly respond.

"When you are adept at *listen and hear* with your whole body, you will recognize the real problems. Time and time again, my training for hospitals and their staff to *listen and hear* has dramatically improved their relationships with patients, resulting in improved patient care and medical outcomes.

"When you are adept at *listen and hear*, you provide your audience with real insights. The ultimate reward is your ability to provide understanding and compassion, resulting in the best possible solutions. Is there a better way than that to stand out in a competitive marketplace?"

"Not that I can think of."

"*Listen and hear* every moment you can."

"I have to ask. How did you and the Sales Guru connect?"

"We went to college together and reconnected years later. He attended a lecture I gave to an executive MBA program at our alma mater. The subject was how to use music to learn to *listen and hear*. He's been working with me ever since."

I am beginning to realize that the Sales Guru is clearly into lifelong learning. Cory, Andrea, and now Ron, have all pointed out their ongoing relationships with him.

"Any other tips?" I ask.

"Visualize using your ears like a zoom microphone when you enter any setting. First, take in the entire room sound and then pan around as you slowly—and I mean slowly—focus in on each person there. Eventually, you will be guided to where to mindfully *listen and hear*.

"In any Face-to-Face encounter, treat each person first as a member of a whole orchestra and second as a musical instrument. When you become skilled at that you will be amazed how much you can learn about them in a blink."

Like the others, Ron hands me a piece of paper. "It was a pleasure meeting you. I hope I get to see you again. Here's your next stop. Remember to *listen and hear*. Remain open to hearing other people."

With that he heads back to the stage.

Listen and Hear

Look and See

Be Mindful

Be Fully Present

No Prejudgment

Relax

Focus

Yes and...

That afternoon. My mouth waters as I pass what seems to be every possible type of restaurant—Portuguese, Japanese, Vietnamese, Italian, Chinese, Mexican, BBQ, seafood, vegetarian. In the middle of this cultural smorgasbord, a marquee stands out. *Improvability*—the name on the sheet that Ron Fiedler gave me.

Beside the entrance to *Improvability*, running up the wall are captioned photographs. They include various scenes of people on stage. At eye level are news clippings with the headlines such as, "Improvability's New Show a Smash Hit."

After a quick read I learn that this is an improvisational theater company. I have never seen a live improvisation performance. What I know about improvisation comes from a TV show. Performers make up stories based on words and suggestions from the audience.

I've gone from mindfulness trainer, to art curator, to orchestra conductor, and now to actors. None of them strike me as having traditional business backgrounds. Yet, they clearly played, and continue to play, an important role in the Sales Guru's success.

My new adventure is to meet with Brent Haley. He greets me in the lobby, wearing baggy jeans, a well-worn black T-shirt with an "Improvability" logo, and scruffy torn sneakers. His curly black hair tops off his skinny frame. I put him in his late thirties or early forties.

"Welcome. Come join us—we're in rehearsal." He leads me into the theater.

Eventually, I learn that his "join us" will become literal.

It is a tiny and dark theater, surrounded on four sides with tiers of empty folding chairs. Four people are in the center of the stage chatting. Two attractive women. A redhead. The other has grey-streaked brown hair. One stocky, bald-headed guy and a muscular man with blond hair. They are as casual, well-worn, and about the same age as Brent. They stop talking when we enter. Brent introduces me and invites me to join the group in their rehearsal.

"Join you?" I ask incredulously. My body tenses. Shock shoots up my spine. I love challenges, but this one intimidates me.

"First of all, I've never even seen an improvisation performance. Although I know what the word improvise means—sort of making it up on the spot. I have no idea how it works. More important, I'm not an actor or a performer."

Brent looks me squarely in the eye, and in his deep resonant voice says, "I thought you were a salesperson."

"Well, yes," I respond.

"I've never met a successful salesperson who isn't a good performer. Let's face it, you're always on stage. You're always in front of an audience. And if you're any good at sales, once you are Face-to-Face with others, isn't your job to engage that audience? Emotionally engage that audience? Effectively connect with that audience? How else do you expect to stand out in this highly competitive and commoditized world?"

He is right.

He locks me in his gaze. "You are about to learn two words that will change your professional and personal life."

I am dumbstruck and intrigued by Brent's statement. "Two words that will change my professional and personal life?" I can't help wonder if this is the *mojo* to which the Sales Guru referred?

"So what do I do?"

"We are starting an improvisation exercise. At an appropriate time, join in. Let's get going. If you're sharp and you **listen and hear** you'll pick it up quickly. Think of it as a form of storytelling, and you are part of a storytelling team."

That I am intimidated is putting it mildly. Brent tells me the idea is to build a sensible story that has a beginning, middle and end working collaboratively by building off each other. The story is to be built on three words—house, cat, and food.

They begin developing a story as they move around the stage, effortlessly and smoothly playing off each other.

I stand like a dummy, trying to figure out what to say when it gets to me, I have no idea when it will be my turn. My mind is churning away, trying to follow the storyline of the cat in the house looking for food. I pray I won't make an ass of myself.

All of a sudden, five of them turn and look at me. I am mute, frozen to the spot. I've lost the thread of the story. With all my mental mumbo-jumbo I can't focus. I am not present and I clearly didn't **listen and hear**.

Brent says, "You weren't present, were you?"

I respond with "No, but...."

Brent abruptly cuts me off. "First of all 'no but' doesn't work here. I'll get back to that in a moment. You met with Cory, Andrea, and Ron didn't you?"

"Yes."

"You were introduced to how to *engage mindfulness*, *look and see*, and *listen and hear*. These are three crucial steps necessary to successfully improvise.

"Whether you're on stage, in a job interview or doing a sales presentation, you need to develop the skills to be fully present and pay attention in the moment, actively looking to see and listening to hear. Forget about what's going on in your head. It is about what's taking place with the person or people in the room. In improvisational theater we take it a step further. The two most important words that form the foundation for improvisational theater are *Yes and*...."

"*Yes and*...?" I question.

Brent rapidly responds, "There are no No's..., no 'No buts'..., no 'Yes buts'..., no 'Yes however'..., or 'However'..., there is only *Yes and*...."

Intrigued, yet bewildered, I say, "Help me to understand *Yes and*...?"

"The principle of *Yes and*... starts with accepting what you're given, acknowledging it, making the other person look good, and doing it for the greater good of the whole. In improvisational theater, one does not anticipate what's going to be said or think about how to respond, change the direction, or preprogram how to take it to another level. You leave prejudgment at the stage door. The goal in improvisation is to build off of each other."

Yes and...
Two words that will change your professional and personal life.

"How does this apply to sales?"

"People new to improvisational theater and learning how to improvise are similar to most people engaged in a sales presentation, business meeting or interview. One is always trying to force the dialogue without paying attention to what's really being said, or not being said. Or paying attention to what's really happening or not happening at the moment. Think of *Yes and...* as accepting an offer and building on it. As in mindfulness, think of it as leaving your mind prepared for the unprepared."

"Yes, but," I start, but Brent jumps in and emphatically reminds me that 'Yes but' doesn't work here!

I think for a moment and start, "*Yes and...* I'm sure if I was an actor like you I would be able to do what you're asking me to do."

Brent tells me that "Acting is a good skill to have even if you're not going on stage. A good acting course will teach you how to use and think with your entire body. If your goal is to be a super salesperson there are lots of basic acting courses out there for people like you. You would greatly benefit from an acting class to learn *whole-body thinking*. To learn how to use and sharpen all five senses along with your sixth mind sense."

I think to myself, here it is again—five senses and mind sense. *Whole-body thinking*.

"I thought acting is when someone plays a character other than him or herself. Are you suggesting that I be someone other than who I am, in order to be successful in sales—that I be phony?"

"Not at all," Brent responds. "What I'm recommending is that you obtain the acting skills necessary to allow you to tap into and use your own innate assets. To succeed in sales you have to know how to improvise, perform and win over an audience. It's about the ability to communicate Face-to-Face and make an effective emotional connection."

"With no acting skills, how can I successfully participate in this exercise with you and your team?"

"Here's what I'd like you to do. It starts with what Cory, Andrea and Ron taught you. ***Engage mindfulness*** to be present in the moment. ***Look and see. Listen and hear.*** Whenever you think you're being passed the story, add the first thing that pops into your mind beginning with the words ***Yes and....*** Also, feel free to enter the improvisation at any time. Always start with ***Yes and....*** We'll model it for you so you can grasp the concept and see how it works. This will help you feel part of the collaboration."

Easier said than done, I think, recalling that trying not to anticipate and clearing monkey chatter out of my head has proven to be daunting tasks these past few days.

My hands start to sweat. My muscles tense. I work hard to be present, and ***listen and hear***. I think it is probably the only thing that will save me from making a complete fool out of myself.

"Okay, I'm ready."

This time around the actors make it clear when they want me to participate. I try to be as innovative and creative as I possibly can, and to build on the storyline they are developing. At one point I juxtapose cat with dog to everyone's amusement.

After about ten minutes I begin to feel a bit more

comfortable. I am amazed that by staying in the present, listening and hearing, I can build on the story without thinking ahead or planning anything to say or do. Frequently, I find I can quickly respond to what I am given and build on it.

A ghost tale about a starving tiger cat wandering around in a cob-webbed and dilapidated haunted house searching for mice is unfolding. Brent speaks, "The cat slinks around the corner and prepares to pounce on the frightened trapped mouse."

The skinny blond male actor says, "Yes, and just then the transparent ghost of a huge black dog grabs the mouse." The red-haired actress continues "from the claws." The Bald male actor adds, "and jaws of the cat." The actress with grey-streaked brown hair jumps in, "The cat freezes. Electrified," and I add, "Yes, and its hairs stand up on end. Not to be denied the cat roars like a lion and distracts the ghostly dog enough to grab the squealing mouse."

Brent stops the exercise and congratulates me on my improvement. "Nice job. *Yes and...*, *Yes and...* and *Yes and...*, he repeats, "Say it out loud until it's etched in your mind. After a while it'll be implied when you respond to someone. That someone could be a prospect, client, significant other, spouse, friend, child or partner. With enough practice there won't be a need to say *Yes and...* out loud.

Yes and...

He goes on to say, *"Yes and...* will change your life

significantly and dramatically. It will improve your ability to build and strengthen your relationships. ***Yes and...*** only works when you ***engage mindfulness, look and see*** and ***listen and hear***. Only then you will know what's given to you so you can fully accept it. Once you acknowledge that, you build on it to make the other person look good, and do it for the greater good of the whole. This is the foundation of improvisation. It is then you will make the effective emotional connection you are looking for—in your case, getting to yes in a sale."

"Thank you Brent—I get it."

This exercise with Brent and his troupe clears up any confusion I have regarding my prior meetings with Cory, Andrea, and Ron. The Sales Guru is putting me through a process that makes more sense with each new step. The concept of ***Yes and...*** fascinates me."

I am beginning to grasp what the Sales Guru meant when he told me that I need to conquer the wind within me. I'm starting to realize that I am my own master. That I just may possess the innate assets and untapped resources to stand out and achieve all my desired goals. I am realizing I lack the skill sets to do that. Now I need to find the way to develop into that master. Perhaps this is the path.

"You're welcome to take classes with us," Brent offers. "That's what the Sales Guru did. He came to one of our performances. He had read about our classes for businessmen, and turned out to be one of our best students. He told us that often in a meeting or presentation, when it didn't go the way he expected, he had to improvise on the spot."

"You are so right. Recently, I prepared for an hour-long presentation with a CEO, only to be informed at the outset he could only spare fifteen minutes. I wish I had had better improvisation skills at that meeting."

Brent continues, "Maybe you will have the opportunity to develop those skills and to learn how the concept of *Yes and...* keeps the Sales Guru on the successful path to continually get to yes.

"At one point we asked him if he would—on occasion—perform with us. He declined saying he gets more than enough opportunity to perform and improvise as a salesperson. Thanks to the Sales Guru we have an active business of training sales teams and business development professionals at major companies in the concept of *Yes and....*"

"I would like to develop improvisational skills. What's the chance of working with you?" I scan the faces of the other actors and the empty chairs in the theater waiting for an answer.

Brent looks at me for a moment and says, "That all depends."

That's all he said. It left me hanging there hungering for a better answer.

I am puzzled by what he means by "That all depends."

He reminds me again about *Yes and....*

"You can begin practicing it right away in any—and I mean any—Face-to-Face situation. Accept what you are given, acknowledge it, make the other person look good, and do it for the greater good of the whole. *Yes and...* is the critical step to take in dialogue to enable you to connect emotionally, solidly Face-to-Face."

With that, he wishes me luck, hands me a sheet of paper and expresses his desire—in any event—to see me again for class.

At this point, I am used to someone handing me a piece of paper with instructions for my next step on the journey. This time, the only thing written on the paper is the name Judith Gilman, and a phone number.

My anxiety level and curiosity levels are just as high as they were at the beginning of this journey. Each "teacher" makes me realize I have a lot to learn about myself. It's happening so fast, and in such a condensed time-frame. I can't sort it out or plan my own next steps. However, each of them has shown me a way to drill down and dig deeper to find my own resources.

As I leave the theater, I realize how often I jump the gun to push my agenda in any meeting. Too often I start with the stereotype of what my prospects and the meeting will be like. Little wonder—more often than I like—I have trouble making solid and lasting connections.

Yes and....

Listen and Hear

Look and See

Be Mindful

Be Fully Present

No Prejudgment

Relax

Focus

StorySelling

On one hand, I now realize what habits are holding me back. On the other hand, none of these people appear to have real sales acumen. Again, I wonder if **engage mindfulness, look and see, listen and hear** and **Yes and...** will work in a business environment. I'm not sure, and I definitely don't want to make a fool out of myself trying it.

To go forward, or not to go forward? How many more steps along this path will I be so unceremoniously passed on? I have no idea. How these pieces come together is still a mystery to me. A bigger mystery for me is: Do I have what it takes to conquer the wind within me? Changing limiting habits is long hard work.

I stare at the paper Brent just handed to me. Putting it on the car seat, I try to think of alternatives to taking any next steps on this journey.

Impulsively, I take three deep breaths as I sit in my car. My shoulders start to relax. The tension in my neck eases. Slowly, as I keep breathing in and out, my mind clears as the sun warms my face. For a moment I can sense the wind within me dying down. Then I remember what brought me to the Sales Guru in the first place. What has kept me on this journey he's sent me on. He is the best-of-breed with decades of proven success. And I'm meeting with the people who helped him.

Finally, I pick up the paper and dial the number. A clear, rich, melodic voice answers. "Hi, you've reached Judith Gilman, what's your story?" I am about to respond when I realize it is a voice message. I give my name and start leaving my number when I hear the phone being picked up and a voice says, "So darling, I am Judith.

I've been expecting you. What's your story?"

"What's my story?" I ask. "I'm not sure what you mean."

"You'll find out soon enough. So darling, here are the directions to my studio. See you tonight at seven."

Step-by-step, with in-depth descriptions of significant landmarks, she details my route to her studio.

"What kind of studio?" I ask.

"A studio is a studio. You've seen one you've seen them all." She says in a sing-song pattern. "I'll see you at seven. Enjoy the scenery."

This woman has a wry sense of humor. Each new person has been fascinating. Once again, I'm game for another adventure.

I follow her directions to the North Shore of Boston and end up at a huge, multi-color, gingerbread Victorian house. It reminds me of the San Francisco homes often referred to as the "Painted Ladies." The house is intense yellow with turquoise, pink and black trim. It sticks out from the rest of the neighborhood. I begin to wonder what kind of character lives in a house like this. What will Judith Gilman be like?

As I approach the massive paneled wooden door, it swings open. A handsome, tall, commanding woman, with long, wavy jet-black hair, dressed in loose jeans and a bright yellow and raspberry sweatshirt emblazoned with the words "Sharing the Fire" across the front, waves me to come in.

"So darling, you met the Sales Guru. You are lucky. There must be something special about you. He is very selective. Have you enjoyed your visits with Cory, Andrea, Ron and Brent?"

I take a breath, "What's clear is I have a lot to learn. After my improvisation lesson with Brent, I believe I'm getting a sense of where all this could lead."

"Yes, and that's why you're here. To learn how it all comes together." Judith says matter-of-factly.

I still have no idea who Judith is, what she does, or how she fits into this journey. She is a jovial character, with a deep captivating voice and engaging manner. I sense I'm going to enjoy this particular experience.

She leads me into a large oak-paneled room with floor-to-ceiling bookcases. The walls above the low paneling are covered in deep green velvet material. There is a large lime-green backdrop hanging on its own frame at one end of the room. Opposite the backdrop at the other end of the room is a video camera mounted on a tripod. The outside wall of the room contains a huge marble fireplace. Opposite the fireplace is a large brown leather couch. Next to it is a stately yet comfortable-looking red-leather wing-back chair. Looking at the video camera and backdrop I wonder if this is to be my big screen test.

We sit down. Judith asks me, "So what's your story?"

So what's your story?

"I'm not sure what you mean," I blurt out.

"We all have scores of personal stories in our internal database, comprised of all the bits and bytes of memory that we've accumulated since birth. Those are the stories. Tell me one of your stories," she insists.

So I start telling her the story of my life. I begin

with where I was born, followed by my educational background, and then I list my career goals and recent jobs.

"Boring, darling, boring. You're so like many business people. I didn't ask for a chronological history. I want a story, a colorful story, which enables me to get to know you. I want an emotional story which will touch me and allow me to relate to you—to connect with you. This isn't rocket science. We're talking relationship-building here. That's what sales is all about isn't it? Sell me on *you,* darling," she urges.

My head is filled with babble. I have no idea how to tell an "emotional story." I can't remember the last time I thought about things in my personal life that would be of interest to anyone, especially a sales prospect. What does this woman do, I wonder?

I turn to her and ask, "Who are you? What do you do? Why am I here?"

"Now you're asking me for a story. Nope! Your price of admission to my life is to tell me a colorful and emotional story about you."

I rack my brain to think of something that will interest her.

Finally, I remember a recent deal I put together. I tell her about the problem this customer was experiencing, and how my company's services helped solve the problem. I explain our client's product, their manufacturing process, and the snafu they were having with their component suppliers.

I tell her how, after simple implementation of my company's software, the client gained complete overview, on an hour-to-hour basis, of what was happening in their supply chain.

"Boring, darling, boring!" she retorts. "That story couldn't get you admission to a free concert. It's all boring facts with no human interest and absolutely no emotional content whatsoever."

My ego deflates like a balloon stuck with a pin.

"Tell me a story in a way that makes me **look and see** and **listen and hear**. Engage me. Pull me into your present moment," demands Judith.

With a surge of defiance I look into her dark brown eyes and say, "You told me if I told you a story you would tell me yours. I told you one. Your turn!"

Her eyes twinkle. She shifts in the red-leather chair. "You're a piece of work," she says.

"So anyway," she continues, "I'll give you an example. I grew up in an old brown clapboard house. Not as fancy as this one, but warm and comfortable. Every night, sitting in our tiny living room, in a well-worn, high-backed wing chair upholstered with a faded purple flower pattern, and surrounded by an abundance of old sepia, black-and-white and color family photographs, I cuddled in my mother's lap as she told me a story. Mum was a tiny, attractive, and strong woman. Her grey hair was pulled into a bun. A very, very, wise, kind and gentle person she was, giving and forgiving. Her constant smile lit up a room. Her stories were filled with humor, danger, challenges, and successes. They were stories about people overcoming challenges.

"Occasionally, she'd throw in a story about animals, and on rare occasions a fantasy tale. As I think back, her constant theme was that we have the power, talent and resources within us to fully realize many of our goals and dreams.

"As Mum told her stories I visualized everything she described in my mind's eye.

"My Mum painted with words. This enabled me to create vivid images in my mind of everything she portrayed. She was the ultimate storyteller.

"It wasn't until I was seven or eight years old that I realized many of the stories she made up on the spot. She was so gifted. I can't recall her ever repeating a story. Every story was different. Every story was a lesson in life and success."

As I sit here listening to Judith, hearing her captivating voice with all the subtle variations of a full orchestra and her movements and facial gestures, highlighting the key points, I am transported back attempting to recall my childhood.

I can't remember a time when anybody in my family ever read me a story. Our lives were very linear. Time was spent watching television and playing video tapes, engaged in computer games, listening to my father's repetitive war stories about his business ventures.

Judith continues, "As I got older I realized the impact of storytelling and its ability to build an emotional connection between the teller and the listener. I miss my mother. She passed away a few years ago. However, she is still with me. In an instant, I can bring her and her stories back. The strongest words my mother left me with were the closing words for most of her stories. Two consistent points. 'Be true to yourself and never give up.'

"The bond my Mum and I have is the same bond you can build with others—even strangers—through storytelling. The Sales Guru calls it StorySelling."

She is the ultimate storyteller.

I am warming up to Judith, but still have no idea of who she is or what she does. At the same time, I desperately try to be fully present in the moment—with purpose. If nothing else, my prior visits with Cory, Andrea, Ron and Brent keep me wanting to be mindful in any and all situations.

I turn to Judith and say to my surprise, "Yes, and thank you for that story, it was touching. I envy you having that opportunity. Clearly it had an impact on your life. I never had that chance. Please, tell me more about the Sales Guru and StorySelling."

She smiles at me with a big broad smile. "'**Yes and...**' huh. Very impressive. I see you did learn something after all."

"Yes, and," I go on, "besides learning more about StorySelling I want to know more about you and the role you play or played in the Sales Guru's life."

"Nice touch with the '**Yes and...**'" affirms Judith. "Brent clearly had an impact on you."

A sense of accomplishment shot through me. "Yes, and I appreciate your compliment. Now please tell me who you are and what you do."

"I'm a professional storyteller," she says cheerily. "In addition to performing, I coach and train a variety of people in storytelling. Most of my clients are corporate executives and sales and business development professionals in major companies."

"Which is it: StorySelling or storytelling, and why

is it an important step in becoming a top salesperson?"

"It doesn't matter if you're selling a product or service, serving a client, courting a partner, or dealing with children, the way to make a lasting impression is to make an emotional connection. StorySelling is how to do that. Let's face it, darling, in today's commoditized marketplace, there are a number of people who can do exactly what you can do, as well as you can do it.

"The real key to standing out is that *you*—your persona—is the only differentiator. It is really all about YOU connecting with others. They need a reason to connect with YOU. A fully realized and well-told story invokes the six senses in your audience so they can visualize what you say. People will retain more from a mental image than from any PowerPointless image. Emotionally connected mental images are the key to getting to yes. That's where storytelling comes in."

People will retain more from a mental image.

"Well, it sounds well and good," I start. Judith cuts me off, "It's better than well and good. Corporate executives across the country are being coached in storytelling. Sales and business development teams for Fortune 500—no change that to Fortune 100 companies—are being coached in storytelling. They're learning how to draw upon their own personal stories, company stories and professional experiences, and how to use them as metaphors that parallel the business situations they find themselves in.

"Once an audience can create mental images and internalize your ideas in context with their life experiences, it shortens the route for you to get the yes.

"StorySelling brings into play the combination of storytelling, improvisation, and acting. These three ingredients have a common structure, a structure designed to help the recipients of the story create a vivid picture in their minds as you paint your story. That's the beginning of how to make an emotional connection. You will learn that most people base their decisions first on emotion, then on facts to support those decisions."

You will learn that most people base their decisions first on emotion, then on facts to support those decisions.

Fascinated, I ask, "What is this common structure?"

"Do you know what mise en scène means?" she asks me.

"I have no idea."

"In a play, film, TV show, an improvisation piece or a novel, mise en scène is describing the full picture of the setting or location. You describe by verbally painting the location so listeners can visualize the scene in their mind. Mise en scène is a French term referring to the setting. That's part of what you worked on with Andrea."

"Okay, mise en scène, I get it. Visualize, then describe the entire setting. Let me try. I am sitting in a magnificent, wood-paneled library, with green velvet walls above the paneling. Filling the walls are generations of large and small framed photographs of family scenes. The furniture is oversized and well-worn. A roaring fire lights up the knickknacks in the room...."

"Enough being a smart aleck," quips Judith. "Obviously, you get it. Once the general scene is set in detail, you focus on the characters. When you fully describe the character physically and emotionally, the visualization will be stronger for the listener.

"The classical structure of a dramatic work began with Aristotle, in ancient Greece, and it still holds true today. It starts out with exposition that describes the location, the scene, the characters and the challenges. Then there comes rising action—running into obstacles or challenges. The turning point, crisis or climax culminates at the height of the rising action, where a decision has to be made on how to overcome the obstacles or challenges. After which there is falling action as the resolution develops and ends up with the denouement— the revelation, resolution and conclusion."

"That could make for a long story in the sales setting."

Judith answers with, "All you do for sales is simplify classical dramatic structure and determine the point you want to make, which is as good as it gets. It goes like this. Paint the picture of the location. Describe the characters. Present the challenge, and the obstacles in the way of achieving the goal. Describe at what critical point the obstacles were overcome and how the goal was reached, what the resolution was. With experience you can condense a compelling story into a few minutes.

"To be successful at StorySelling, you need to incorporate all the pointers, recommendations and suggestions that you received from Cory, Andrea,

Ron, Brent and me. Don't forget it's about being fully engaged, using all six of your senses, and thinking, working and speaking with your entire body so that you can *engage mindfulness, look and see, listen and hear* and use *Yes and...* to improvise with an appropriate metaphorical story that makes your point."

Thinking for a moment, I respond, "My concern is that it doesn't leave much room for explaining the feature/function of a product or service."

"By utilizing a good story as a metaphor you will make the selling point." Judith pauses, "Three things will result from StorySelling. One, you emotionally connect with the listener. Two, they get a clear picture that you understand the problems they are facing. And three, you are well on your way to building their confidence that you can provide them with a solution necessary for you to get them to yes. Remember, people aren't seeking your ideas; they are not looking for feature/function; they want your insight into their problems."

People are not looking for feature/function. They want your insight into their problems.

Judith continues, "I believe that every person has enough life experiences or company stories that can be translated into metaphors paralleling the situation they face in order to get to yes. Be sure to do it in a very illustrative and colorful way to emotionally engage the listener or listeners. You want them to visualize and internalize your information."

"I don't have those kinds of personal stories. What if I adapt case studies in my industry?"

Judith smiled and took a deep breath. "Let's think about the story you told me about a client who had a supply chain problem that your company was able to resolve. And when you think about that story, work on telling it using the classic dramatic structure. Let me show you how.

"First use your inner-vision to visualize your experience. Then describe the physical setting. *It is a rundown, dilapidated old mill building. I'm in the cluttered office of the CEO of a family-owned business. File boxes and papers are everywhere.* Describe the client physically and emotionally in detail and what keeps him up at night. *The CEO is in his forties. Thinning brown hair and lifeless eyes. He is dressed in the traditional blue, pinstriped suit. His face—strained, grey and gaunt—is in sharp contrast to his bright red tie.* Be dramatic in portraying the challenge, goal and obstacle. *Anxious and stressed, he is faced with meeting a huge order deadline. Meeting that deadline would provide the necessary cash to save the company from closing and eliminating 47 jobs. He says he can't sleep at night. Panicked, he needs to quickly develop a consistent and coordinated flow of materials from three suppliers.* Explain in non-technical detail how you defined and then solved the problem and the impact the solution had on the client emotionally and then fiscally. *Step-by-step, I show him how my company can provide—quickly and cost-effectively—a software supply-chain solution that will give him and his executives a real-time overview of the entire material flow from suppliers to their manufacturing operation. Strapped for cash, he vacillates for over a week in making decision to sign with us. Growing more desperate to save his company, he finally uses his personal funds to engage us. Our software quickly and easily integrates with their legacy enterprise programs without causing interference with existing operations. Within a month of going live with our program, they were able to effectively and efficiently manage the supplier-to-manufacturing process. In the end, my client saved his company—47 jobs!—and he slept at night because he met the delivery deadline with room to spare. Now he is a healthier CEO—with color in his face matching his red tie—as a result of an increased profit margin thanks to our solution.* That's StorySelling with color. The alternative in this case would be to find a parallel metaphorical story in your life experience database to make the same point."

"Again, I say, I don't think I have them."

Judith makes a silly face and says, "Let's face it darling, life is a series of metaphors. Think of where we'd be if we can be fully present at the time they occur, be aware enough to recognize them, capture them and then develop the ability to recall them from our mind's database and visualize them in full color in our mind's eye."

Life is a series of metaphors.

"Any suggestions as to how I get there?" I reply.

"Yes, to build trust and belief while StorySelling, start by sharing what motivates you. Tell in—full Technicolor—what shaped your life that specifically relates to the situation you are in presently. Express your point of view and what you care about through your story. Build trust.

"Face-to-Face success takes a number of skills. You have been exposed to five skills sets to get you there. Use them and practice, practice, practice."

Abruptly she says, "So darling, we are done. Your next stop is back with the Sales Guru. You are expected at 10 o'clock tomorrow morning."

"Seeing him is something I truly look forward to. I have so many questions for him."

"Yes, and I advise you to take the time between now and then to reflect on all that you experienced with the five of us. Practice what you can and see that you put it all together into a wonderful story. Maybe by doing that, you will emotionally connect with the Sales Guru."

"I didn't see any emotion in him when we met," I say.

"Yes, and maybe you weren't fully present. Think about that," she sharply responds, pauses, and then warmly concludes, "So darling, it's been nice meeting you. You aren't as boring as many. If you pass the test I'm sure I'll see you again." And with that, she walks me to the door and says goodbye with a big smile on her face.

StorySelling

Yes and....

Listen and Hear

Look and See

Be Mindful

Be Fully Present

No Prejudgment

Relax

Focus

Reflections/Thoughts

She is quite a character. I wonder what test she's referring to. Dammit! I didn't find out how she and the Sales Guru connected.

As I walk to my Audi, I think of my experiences over the past few days. I realize how little of my life I bring to my work. This is an exciting way to approach sales presentations. I got so caught up in the belief that harnessing social media was the key for success.

Hmm. Corporate executives being trained in storytelling. Corporate executives learning improvisation. Law enforcement agencies and personnel, judges, the army, learning to *engage mindfulness*, going to museums to learn how to *look and see,* hospital personnel being taught on how to *listen and hear.* I'm beginning to realize why the old ways don't work anymore. This journey is fascinating. And a lot to absorb.

The old ways don't work anymore.

None of this is what I expected. This is new and exciting stuff. Now, if only I can conquer the wind within me.

Curt, Andrea, Ron, Brent and Judith make sense. I see how the ability to effectively communicate Face-to-Face can exponentially enhance the successes we gain by using social media to make an initial connection.

Yes, they are an eclectic group, who had and still exert a major influence on the Sales Guru's life and successes.

I remember the red light approach as I drive back

to my hotel. Every time I come to a red light I practice three breaths in and out. On the way, I stop at a bookstore to purchase a few books and CDs on meditation and mindfulness training.

By the time I arrive at my hotel, I'm ready for a substantial New England lobster dinner with melted butter, sweet corn, all the fixings and a frosted glass of cold beer.

The Sales Guru

Overnight I gave a lot of thought to what I learned and experienced meeting the Sales Guru's teachers.

My heart is pounding with excitement, as I am shown into his office the next morning by the auburn-haired, perky, and tastefully dressed receptionist Maria. The Sales Guru is already sitting at his handcrafted oak desk. The sun is pouring in the window just over his right shoulder. It backlights his wild white hair. As before, dressed in all black, he sits there and stares at me. His daunting appearance creates a magical and ominous quality.

As this point I've learned not to speak until spoken to. This silent time is the time I am supposed to be listening to my breath and becoming fully present in the moment. It is a struggle for me. I am anxious. I want to be taken under his wing.

Finally, he asks me, "What did you learn about yourself?"

All night and early this morning all I could think about was what was he going to ask me and what answers I could provide. This definitely was not the question I expected. As if on cue, the monkey chatter floods my brain.

What do I say? What is he looking for? I have no idea what to say.

The Sales Guru looks at me kindly and says, "Take two minutes to listen to your breath. Clear your mind. Become present. Practice overcoming your bad habit energy. I assume by now that you know what habit energy is."

Chastened, I nod. "Yes, and based on what I've learned the past few days," I blurt out, "It'll take me some time to learn to overcome my habit energy."

"Well said," he responds. "Then I see you did learn something. I like the *Yes and...*, nice touch."

"I'm not sure what you mean by that."

I'm locked in his gaze as he says, "This is about you. It's not about me. Do you remember what I said, when we first met? What works for me won't necessarily work for you. Each of us possesses a creative capacity, along with all the innate resources we need to be successful. Once you find them, and recognize them, you'll fire your passion. You are your own master.

"It's about being all that you truly are capable of. Therein lies one of the challenges—who are you, what are your personal assets? You share the same problem as the Archer. Once you learn to conquer the wind within you, you will take a major step in order to move forward."

The Sales Guru continues, "It took me a while to realize how stuck I was in my ways. I based my drive to be successful on my personal desires. Unfortunately, it took me a long time to learn what is important are the needs of those I'm addressing. My arsenal of solutions often didn't match the problems of the people I was meeting. I had to undo years of rushing to present my agenda instead of taking the time to listen to others. That took a lot of hard work. Seeking to *listen and hear* to understand the problems of others began to pay dividends as I worked with my mentor group."

I think for a moment and say, "From what I experienced the last few days it appears that in order to conquer the wind within me I need to learn how to be mindful instead of mindless."

"Yes, and first you need to dig deep and define and then mine what makes you unique. You need to work on listening to your inner voice. I don't believe you can hear it yet. Think about it. When it comes to Face-to-Face, you possess the most powerful social media tool of all. YOU!

"You see, negative habit energy is not entirely your fault. It comes from a never-ending commentary that begins at a very early age.

"I grew up in a tiny, crowded fourth-floor tenement apartment in the West End of Boston. Today, my street is gone, replaced with luxury high-rise condos. Anyway, my parents couldn't afford much. When I was four, my favorite activity was drawing pictures with the Crayola crayons they bought me. That was until the day my uncle commented on my latest creation of a landscape. 'Skies aren't pink they're blue. You don't want people to make fun of you because you draw pink skies. Skies are blue.' That was one of my earliest experiences with the linear thinking pattern that haunted my entire education from kindergarten through college and my early work life in companies. A continuous patter of 'no you can't, here's the answer.' 'Fear the judgment of others.' 'Don't make mistakes.' 'Be serious.'

"That is the linear educational system and work environment I referred to at our first meeting."

He goes on, "All this negative linear thinking has been drilled into us at every step of our lives, forming the bad habits now ingrained in us. We are well-trained in self-doubt and self-scrutiny. We are afraid to step out of our comfort zones. We fear the judgment of others. We lack the ability to focus on self-awareness.

"Education as we know it today drains our confidence and strip-mines our use of the right brain. These are the habits that you and others like you need to change into creative thinking, critical problem-solving, and collaboration.

"One day, at work, I woke-up and realized my uncle was wrong. Skies can be whatever color you want them to be. Tired of being like everyone else I decided that life on a roller coaster could be more exciting and could provide greater rewards than life on a merry-go-round. I learned since then that I made the right choice."

Wanting to hear more, I ask, "So what did you do?"

The Sales Guru shifts in his chair and continues, "To be successful, I had to reprioritize some of the basic characteristics I possessed. I learned that we have three basic personality traits. The traits of the champion, the critic and the brat. At any given time, one of these characteristics can dominate. The goal is to learn how to bring out your champion and control your critic and particularly your brat. One needs to develop the skills to be the champion as much as one can."

"What do you mean by champion, critic, and brat?"

"Well," he responds, "the champion is that personality in us where we know who we are, and that we are good at what we do. We are confident. We feel good about ourselves. We recognize our value. The critic refers to the self-critic within. It's the character that constantly puts us down, that inner voice that makes us focus on and fear the judgment of others. It's our low self-esteem. The brat is the most destructive of all. The brat is the egomaniac within us. It says, 'been-there-done-that—nobody can teach me anything new. I'm better than anybody else.'

"Once we stop fearing the judgment of others, the more confident and successful we will become. To accomplish that I had to step outside my comfort zone and turn limiting habits into creative thinking on how I could stand out."

He pauses and looks at me intensely, and then asks, "So right now, who is dominating you?"

"I'm not sure. I'm not sure which personality my utter confusion fits into. There is one question hanging over me since I met your teachers, mentors or whatever you call them. Why didn't you start me with the storyteller? That way the rest of the steps would have made more sense to me."

"Is your brat dominating you right now?" he asks. "Do you prefer the quick solution?"

"I don't think it's my brat, it's my curiosity to understand why," I reply.

"The road to change years of bad habits is extremely difficult and takes considerable time. To effect personal change and build something durable requires solid footing. You needed the basic steps in order to grasp the principles of StorySelling."

He pauses, "What I developed and call 'The Five Steps' give me the skills to be successful in business. They provide me with the ability to live a fuller and richer life. They are the tools and techniques to aid you in overcoming all the ingrained behavior you've developed over a lifetime. It's time to get off the speed road—the Autobahn to nowhere. It's time to learn how to be effective, as opposed to efficient."

"I definitely desire to be more effective," I interject. "I can't see anybody in today's society walking away from or discounting the benefits of technology."

The Sales Guru shot right back at me, "Yes, and we are churning out generations of people who are whizzes at text messaging and video games while doing a multitude of other activities. Everyone is chattering but I wonder who, if anyone, is really listening? The result is we have two generations nowhere near ready to cope with the global human challenges of the 21st century."

Everyone one is chattering but I wonder who, if anyone, is really listening?

"Your journey involved exposure to the five steps for professional or personal success. The necessary steps to successfully get the sale. Each step carries a great benefit. I found that collectively they are my most effective sales tools."

"The five steps?" puzzled I ask, "What are the steps?

After a moment, the Sales Guru begins, "It all started with neuroscience. I read an article about brain studies that shows the more we are in touch with all five of their senses, the more agile and imaginative our thinking becomes. Additionally, there is now neuroscience research that proves that the brain can be rewired at any age through new experiences and new activities. It is called neuroplasticity."

"Then there is hope for me!"

He smiles, takes a moment and continues, "That

rewiring has a lot to do with what is being defined as whole-brain thinking. People are trying to break away from linear, sequential, analytical and logical thinking, which is attributed to the left hemisphere of your brain, and start using more of the right hemisphere of the brain for more facile, imaginative, empathetic, innovative and creative thinking. It's not about making left-brain thinkers into right-brain thinkers. It is about showing people how to use more of the right brain."

"Experience is the best teacher," I mutter.

"Like you," he continues, "I went through all the popular sales training programs. Training, for the most part, focused on tactics and techniques—very linear left-brain thinking and cookie-cutter training. All the closes were ingrained in me—part of my DNA—the 'Close' ladder from the Assumptive Close through Puppy Dog Close, up to the Window of Opportunity Close. My favorite at the time was the Provocative Close.

"Still, I wasn't satisfied. I wanted to have a unique, competitive edge. I thought about the neuroscience studies I had read, and how I could apply those concepts to improve my skills in sales.

"At the same time, I became aware of mindfulness training and its significant role in approving one's ability to pay attention fully—to communicate and make decisions more effectively. One day at the gym, I met Cory Stewart and discovered that he was a mindfulness trainer. And so I began training with him, and I've been able to be present ever since.

"There are a few popular training programs that lightly touch upon how to make an emotional connection. If they do, their focus is more on psychological analysis than on providing the tools to enable a person like you to learn how to make the emotional connection. So often, they are so psychologically deep that most people tend to go through them by the numbers and pay little attention to them afterwards.

"Let me come back to your question as to why I started your passage to what I have coined as StorySelling.

"Successful StorySelling requires a strong intra and interpersonal foundation. Any good performer needs all six senses finely tuned. Reflect on the 'Five Steps' as rungs on the ladder to personal satisfaction and success—the building blocks to get to yes."

Frustrated by his constant referral to the "Five Steps" I ask, "But what are the 'Five Steps'?"

"They are steps to reawaken your right brain—the creative hemisphere of the brain," he responds. "They are the tools to tune your instrument—YOU! It's a way to look within and trust yourself, to connect with that part of your brain that supports your creative thinking— your ability to synthesize rather than analyze, your ability to recognize context instead of text.

"As I said earlier, neuroscience has shown that the more you're in touch with all five senses and the right hemisphere of your brain, the more facile, imaginative and creative your thinking is. It is the right hemisphere of your brain that also supports your emotional and creative thinking. Whole new worlds open up for you when you break free from habit energy."

"On one hand you talk about the 'Five Steps'," I exclaim, "on the other hand, you talk about the five senses. I'm confused."

"The 'Five Steps' are the building blocks that

you went through over the past few days: ***Engage Mindfulness, Look and See, Listen and Hear, Yes and..., and StorySelling***. The first four steps provide you with the skills necessary to blink and quickly assess any situation in which you find yourself. They enable you to effectively connect with others emotionally, and finally StorySell."

"Okay, okay, now that you've explained it I can appreciate the value of the sequence."

"Years of experience will eventually give you that ability to blink. You need that ability particularly when you're in a room filled with a diverse audience, so that you can quickly determine the underlying motivations of those present. Then you're able to create a story that will resonate for most of them. That assessment enables you to determine which of your metaphorical stories will fit the circumstances. Many who use a form of storytelling too frequently log into a few repetitive stories that most often are not appropriate for the situation."

"What about the five senses?" I ask.

"The five senses are look and see, listen and hear, breathe and smell, eat and taste, and touch and feel. Hopefully, you'll learn the benefits of ***whole-body thinking*** with the addition of mind sense and discover that the senses make cents."

The senses make cents.

"It is important for you to understand that each training in itself brings great value. However, they are the ingredients for the magic sauce in the order they were presented. It's the *mojo* that gives me my competitive edge that gets me to close the sale."

"Please tell me more!" I implore him.

"For example, I eventually learned that to **engage mindfulness** gave me the ability to walk into a room and quickly sense what was going on for the individuals in that room. Then I discovered that once I added the abilities to **look and see**, **listen and hear**, and incorporate **Yes and...** I could exponentially increase my ability to connect with everyone—and I mean everyone—in the room. So often we don't really pay attention and we end up missing the person or persons who we really needed to focus on. Too frequently, the decision-maker is not the person we set the meeting with. Those four skill sets enable me to select an effective story to **StorySell**."

That makes a lot of sense I think to myself. I realize how ill-equipped I am presently to be best-of-breed.

Turning to the Sales Guru, I say, "Meeting your mentors was not what I expected. It's quite an eclectic group. Yet, I never got a sense that any of them has a strong business background."

The Sales Guru chuckles and responds with, "You met my mastermind group. We meet every month with no agenda except to be supportive, to help everyone stay on track for the goals we've set for ourselves, and to be very candid. We are successful at that because we've been meeting for a long time. I often refer to them as my Board of Directors. My only regret is we didn't begin meeting decades earlier. Their counsel is as important to me as the skill sets each of them brings to the table."

A bit puzzled, I ask, "How so?"

"Those of us in business tend to be myopic."

"I'm not sure I understand what you mean by

myopic."

"When meeting with a group of business peers or a group of salespeople, we too often are set in our ways. Even today, most business people rarely move outside of their comfort zones. It is what I call single vision—myopic. The concept 'if it ain't broke don't fix it' is a very popular one in business. Business people are not great innovative thinkers.

"Each member of my mastermind group comes from a completely different field outside what most would call normal business channels. The result is we each bring different ideas, and experiences and challenges. These folks keep me on track. I deeply respect their opinions."

"You make me wish I had a mastermind group."

"I recommend you immediately build your mastermind group. Find five or six people you trust. Seek people of all ages, people who share your values and come from different professions. Pick people whose advice you respect and who you will listen to. Remember, listening to yourself and questioning yourself deprives you of objective answers."

"Let's come back to the 'Five Steps.' Why haven't I come across them before, or at least heard about them?"

The Sales Guru sits quietly for a moment and says, "In this age of push-button communications and digital embarrassment, I realized that it was time for me to share this with others. Over and over again, I run into people who lack even reasonable Face-to-Face skills. I determined the best way for me to share this would be to become a mentor to others."

"Does that mean that you will mentor me?" I ask

quite excited.

There was a long pause. I went for the three breaths, but ran into a lot of gibberish instead. Will he or won't he? I hope he will. He has to. I'm convinced that he can help me.

"Corey, Andrea, Ron, Brent and Judith are all in agreement that you possess the necessary qualities to grow and become extremely successful. Their collective assessment is that you are personable. You're a quick study and extremely bright. You're open to learn. They sense your passion to excel. They also believe you'll eventually pass the skills they teach you on to others.

"I trust the judgment of my mastermind group, and if you're willing to do the work, I and the others will mentor you. Don't ever forget for a moment, you are embarking on a major undertaking. Understand the power of one. Make the commitment to pay it forward. As I do with you, commit to share what you learn by mentoring others."

You will learn that when it comes to Face-to-Face communications, you are the master of the most powerful social media tool of all.
YOU!

Harness the Wind Within You.

StorySelling

Yes and....

Listen and Hear

Look and See

Be Mindful

Be Fully Present

No Prejudgment

Relax

Focus

Pay it Forward

I think back on how a simple phrase *Yes and...* and the word blink dramatically impacted my life.

It's been years since my first meeting with the Sales Guru. Nervous, filled with anticipation, I sat in his office with no idea of the impact and influence he was to have on my life. Yes! He became my mentor, and remains a close friend.

The months immediately following my initial introductory meetings with Cory, Andrea, Ron, Brent, and Judith made me fully aware of the wind within me that I needed to conquer. I considered myself an A player. My mentors made me realize that I was a B player with A player potential. They taught me what to do to truly achieve A status.

The Sales Guru was a compassionate taskmaster, as were his mastermind group once we began working together. They taught me that it was important to first come Face-to-Face with myself. They taught me how to look in the mirror to see myself for who I was. It was the key to developing the skill-sets to communicate and emotionally connect Face-to-Face with others.

Month after month, I slowly discovered each of the bad habit energy traits that have been getting in my way for so many years.

Being a *Type A* personality (at least I thought so at the beginning) initially made it difficult for me to stop the mental multitasking and gibberish in my head. It took hard work and a considerable amount of practice. The more I practiced, the more I realized the payoff of being mindful and fully present in front of someone else.

I learned how to perceive with greater accuracy by not prejudging or being judgmental with others. My overall effectiveness dramatically increased as I decreased multi-tasking.

It became apparent to me that being mindful instead of mindless was the crucial step in fully engaging with the Sales Guru's 'Five Steps.'

Even today, every time I come to a red light I take three breaths. I don't rush to answer the phone on the first ring. I take deep breaths. Before I push the mental button that activates my mouth, I take a deep breath.

Knowing how to *engage mindfulness* to be fully present in the moment with purpose contributes to my success in all my relationships. This combined with developing the skills to effectively *look and see,* and *listen and hear* increased my ability to "blink" in most situations—to accurately take in the scene before me. Perception was no longer deception. I now know how to *look and see* what is actually before me.

Two words did in fact change my life. *Yes and...* is the best connector anyone can use. Those two words taught me how to accept what I was given by others. It taught me how to respect the opinions and concerns of others in my professional and especially in my personal life.

Storytelling—or as the Sales Guru constantly reminds me, StorySelling—became my most effective tool to emotionally connect with others. I was amazed by how many stories I had to use as metaphors for numerous sales situations.

StorySelling is my fast track for making an emotional connection to eventually close sales.

I did start my own mastermind group within weeks of my first meeting with Sales Guru. They are the Board of Directors of my life. We share our professional and personal lives with each other, support each other, advise each other and care for each other with compassion and understanding.

Branded in my brain are the Sales Guru's parting words at our first meeting. "Understand the power of one. Make the commitment to pay it forward. As I do with you, commit to share what you learn by mentoring others."

In my reception room someone who reminds me of me when I was her age waits to see me. With great persistence, she convinced me to meet with her. The journey continues.

Pay it forward.

Acknowledgements

Over the years, I have learned from and been influenced by many people who I would like to praise here.

Special praise for my Mastermind Group colleagues—Steve Lishansky, Lynn Robinson and Patti Salvucci—who, over many years of regular and productive monthly meetings, continue to be the best advisors, encouragers, supporters and friends I could ask for.

The focus group from diverse ages, experiences and professions who read and provided valuable feedback on my early drafts of the book Tony Pucillo, Ed Murphy, Joan Miller, Jim Smith, Regina Harris, Jonathan Kondracki, Paul and Jaimie Nederhoed.

Authors Dan Pink, Sir Ken Robinson and Michael Gelb, whose books and talks on the importance of creativity in our society and how to rekindle a creative mind, motivated me to combine my business and arts careers to develop Zoka Training® and start the Zoka Institute.

An economics instructor I had in college (whose name I can't remember) who taught me to live my life so I would never say "I wish I had."

John Talvaccia and Ken Halpern for their ongoing friendship, support and counsel.

My copy editor Stacie Slotnick and advising editor Ellen Hoffman.

Toby Snyder, my humorous "tell it like it is" sister who keeps me realistic.

My former theater colleague and long-time best friend, crusty sage Mort Kaplan, who makes sure that I cross my "T's" and dot my "I's," and not just in my writing.

Drs. Michael Rees, Timothy Murtha and Evangelos Gragoudos, whose skills and caring made it possible for me to be able to still see and to be here to write this book.

My sons Joel, Paul and Michael who are my constant reminders that individuality and creative thinking are the best paths.

And very special praise for

Soulmate, marriage partner and best friend Carol Wintle whose love, support, understanding, encouragement, patience and editorial skills contributed significantly to the completion of this book.

About The Author

For more than 45 years, Larry Blumsack has enjoyed successful parallel careers as a speaker, trainer, coach, serial entrepreneur, educator, writer, radio and television host and commentator, and visual and performing artist. *Face-to-Face* is in his DNA.

As a speaker, consultant, workshop facilitator, and coach, he has trained more than 6000 professionals in the skills included in this book. As a business-to-business matchmaker, he set an average of 100 meetings annually with senior executives in Fortune 1000 companies for his clients, while sharing his successful techniques with business development and sales professionals through workshops and coaching.

In 2006, he founded Zoka Institute to combine his multiple careers into one major program and focus—to use his unique arts-for-business approach to introduce companies and their employees to their full creative and innovative potential.

For over 25 years, Larry Blumsack was a syndicated columnist and feature writer for major publications, and a radio and television commentator and critic on the arts.

Larry Blumsack has also launched and operated businesses in digital imaging, video production, marketing and public relations, and gourmet food. He has numerous credits in theater, radio, film and television as an actor, director, designer, and producer. Northeastern University honored him with the Outstanding Alumni Award in the Arts.

He received his B.A. from Northeastern University and M.A from Emerson College.

For more information visit
www.linkedin.com/larryblumsack

To book Larry for an event go to
www.larryblumsack.com

Have Larry Blumsack
Speak At Your Next Event

Larry Blumsack is available for keynote presentations, workshops full-day seminars and coaching. All of Larry's experiential and interactive presentations are a combination of entertainment, education, and motivation. He uses humor, storytelling and arts-based activities to make his points because emotion is the fast-track to the brain.
Visit www.larryblumsack.com to book Larry for your event.

"You are an agile and superb facilitator and did a tremendous job of bringing out the creative aspects of each individual that I don't think they even realized they possessed. You planted a lot of seeds with your tools and techniques."
—Tony Pucillo, Executive Vice President,
Clean Harbor Environmental Services

"Right after Larry's training program, one of our sales executives landed a meeting with a senior VP at one of the largest financial institutions in the country -an elusive individual he had been chasing for months. ... 'I Blumsacked them'."
—Chris Copley, Vice President of Sales, M Squared

Larry was one of the best presenters we (Entrepreneurs' Organization) have had in a while. He really did a great job. He had an objective and a fun way of getting us to meet that objective - thinking more creatively.
—Tori Stuart, President/Founder Zoe Foods

"The program (21st Century Survival Skills for Business Development and Sales) made me think "outside the box" when approaching business development situations."
—Kerry Hands, Business Development, The Bostonian Group

"His training style was very participatory and makes you challenge how you approach sales in this current environment. I highly recommend participating in one of his trainings."
—Elmer Eubanks, Vice President, Business Development, Citibank

"His on-your-feet training exercises shook me out of my comfort zone and showed how to sell proactively and interactively for best results. I recommend him!"
—Andrew Crain, Managing Director, Tully & Holland

"He has a unique approach to connecting with executives that works and is a good trainer."
—Stan Beal, former VP of Sales, Xelus and Vistaar

Proof

Made in the USA
Charleston, SC
13 October 2010